ABC Your Way from Distress to De-Stress:

A Holistic Guide for Home-based Workers

TONYA D. PARKER

ISBN: 979-8-7224-7633-3

DEDICATION

I first dedicate this book to my friends and family who allowed me to provide healing in the days and months leading up to their transitions. I am grateful to have been chosen to help make your final moments more comfortable: Nancy, Monica, Akilah, Safiya, Malaika, Rev. Bonnie, and of course, my mom, Evelyn. I love you all to infinity and beyond…

My next dedication is to all the corporate, government, and education professionals who allowed me to serve them when they worked in an office building. I send a shout out to those who now work at home in our changing landscape. My heart goes out to the many who lost their job. And for those of you who have returned to the office, I know it's not the same. I feel you all, I miss you all, and may this new chapter be bigger and brighter. Blessings galore and so much more!

CONTENTS

ACKNOWLEDGMENTS

I am going to take time to thank some unsung heroes. The first are folks I have worked beside year end and out, helping to bring some peace and release to the corporate workplace. From messages I have been getting this past year, our former corporate clients are missing us immensely! First is John Lee of Whole Body Concepts, who hired me back in 2001 for the first of twenty years' worth of gigs through his company. Though I have worked for other companies and have acquired my own contracts, John was the spark that ignited decades of healing, allowing me to meet amazing people and make long-lasting friends, as well as pay rent and mortgage, travel the world, buy vehicles, and collect beautiful scarves and pashminas. I will be forever grateful to this generous spirit who never fails to bring joy when we have the pleasure of working together.

Next is Cory Scoggins, whom I met through John. There I was showing up at a hospital with my luxury massage chair, thinking I was something. And I got parked beside this tall, handsome gentleman with a zero-gravity chair for foot reflexology. He was courtly, attentive, skilled, and provided personalized music through headphones. His line was much longer than mine was that day because most of the women headed his way! We have been brother and sister ever since. I appreciate his friendship, and the years of gigs he also sent my way.

Much love to my long-time work partner, Malinda Derr, who signed on with me to do one massage gig many years ago, and later, when I asked her to join me at one of my monthly corporate sites, she gave a ready yes. Over ten years later, we have been massage, recipe, and health tip exchange partners, and we have contracted with the other for various gigs. My, I have missed my rock during this pandemic!

Though I have worked with a lot of healers, I must also shout out Antonio Stephens and Arthur Totten, stalwart friends who have accompanied me several times over the years on various gigs. They both have healing hands and hearts, and I am grateful for them in my life. Gig workers rock!

I am blessed with an abundance of souls who lift me up time and again. One of them is my big sis, Rosalyn Gray, editor extraordinaire, who was "voluntold" to edit this book. It is what bratty little sisters do. Next is another Northern Neck of Virginia native and alum of The College of William & Mary, Regina Brayboy. Regina was the first to volunteer to be an extra set of eyes for this book. As a kindred spirit loving holistic living, she was a blessing, and suggested I include the index found at the back of the book, where readers can reference the chapters that speak to specific issues to address. She also sees a higher vision for this book and the ones she insists need to come behind it. Mega love to my partner, Rev. Anim Bey, who rescued me by designing this beautiful cover and told me to take a seat. Then there is the artistic apple who did not fall far from the tree, our son/sun, Ayod Shuford, who indulged me with a mini photo shoot to produce a photo for the back cover. And to some of my fellow sojourners of Path of the Sacred Heart, thank you for agreeing to serve as additional eyes for this book. Rev. Pamela Allen, Rev. Robert Davis, and Iya Ifunsade aka Patricia—you honor me. Spirit's got my back, front, and sides.

Asé, aho, and amen!

ABC Your Way from Distress to De-Stress: A Holistic Guide for Home-based Workers

PREFACE

Times are not what they used to be. So many of us entered the year 2020, excited with a clear vision of what we wanted to accomplish during the year. We did not foresee a global pandemic and upheaval to our daily lives. The impact has been huge, on so many levels.

One of the largest societal changes has been a shift from going off to work to a whopping forty-two percent of the US labor force now working from home full-time, according to a Stanford University study. That is if we are lucky. Thirty-three percent are not working at all. Millions of women, in particular, left the workforce to return home, according to *Fortune Magazine*. And we have also seen an uptick in the entrepreneurial starting their own businesses from home to adapt. I see a trend that will not end just because the pandemic does. Freedom and flexibility are the new sexy.

I sit somewhere in between those numbers. A proud full-time member of the gig economy since 2007, I have evolved into a part-time gigger at home, relying on electronics to help me create a connection that my hands used to. My bread-and-butter income, corporate massage for Washington, DC area companies, dried up when those companies shuttered and set up their employees at home until some unknown time later in 2021 or until a vaccine is widely available and utilized. My local and destination retreats have been postponed to better times—we hope one can be salvaged later in 2021. My monthly healing events and private clients have been put on hold to protect the health and safety of all involved.

Ironically, the profession I left years ago, psychotherapy, is alive and well these days. The stress of health risk, loss of life of those close to us, lockdown at home, under- or unemployment, loss of homes, and schooling children from home was challenging enough. Then we witnessed and/or experienced the racial unrest and ever-widening political divide leading up to the 2020 elections. As if that was not enough, we entered a new year filled with hope, only to see a President holding on to an office he lost with a vise-like grip, and inciting rioters to storm the hallowed halls of our Capitol Building in Washington, DC. Yep, therapy is a good option if you can get it. I happen to know some other great options, which I will share in the pages to come.

Interestingly, pre-pandemic, I received the inspiration for this book. I was providing seated massage services at a corporate event in September 2019. Who knows why I accepted a gig ninety minutes away? Who knows why I did not build in sufficient time to drive through construction slowdowns? But things happened as they did, and I arrived in the parking garage as my start time was beginning. I made it upstairs and was set up and ready to go five minutes after the hour. Who knows why my first client did not show? All these circumstances led to me accepting a walk-in client seeking a session. Though I was not the only therapist available, I felt bad about arriving late, and was in a space of wanting to compensate. I eagerly waved him over to my massage chair, exchanged introductions, and offered him a seat. As soon as I placed my hands on his tight shoulders, it happened: the download for this book.

I have a multitude of gifts, and intuition is one of them. I often receive information from Spirit by being in proximity with people, especially when touching them. This gift has served me well as a body and energy worker. This was the first time I received so much information directed at me by touching someone else. It was amazing! Here was this part of me, facilitating a powerful healing experience for this unknown man seated on my chair, and another part totally in tune with what was being channeled. During breaks, I used my phone notes to capture the information, which continued to fill in over the course of the next few days.

And did I sit down obediently to write this book at that time? No! I procrastinated writing it, month after month. I was working a lot of gigs. In the in-between, I was traveling almost three hours away to spend time with my mom, who was one month shy of having survived a year in home Hospice care for terminal colon cancer. Life was happening, and the book could wait.

Well, word finally came at the end of January 2020, that my mother's time was drawing near. It was then that I decided to start writing before I went off to sit vigil with her for what turned out to be her final week on this earth. I put in a few good hours of writing before I left to be by her side. By the time I settled back home a couple of weeks later from her celebration of life services, writing was the last thing on my mind. That was February 2020. I barely had time to grieve before COVID-19 took hold of our country and basic survival trumped my grief.

Some months later, when I finally sat down to pull up the book, it was nowhere to be found. By this time, I had switched laptops, but I could not find my book document on either one. I checked flash drives, Dropbox, OneDrive and Google Drive. Nope...nada. OK. Start again, right? No, distractions happened. "Until today," as my former catering client, Iyanla Vanzant would say. Apparently, now is supposed to be the time. Spirit is loud and clear. The knowing is flowing through my blood, burrowing within my bones. And... I serendipitously started helping other author friends promote their books, and I became inspired to take care of me like I have taken care of

them. My partner, Anim, reminded me to feed myself
before I feed others, to give from a place of overflow.
So, my book is ready to emerge, and I feel more
balanced helping others since I am devoting time and
energy to mine, as well.

I am clear that this book has evolved with our
workforce, addressing issues that were not occurring
to this degree in September 2019, or even February
2020. Everything about this book has unfolded in
Divine time, in Divine order. So now I get to be
obedient to Spirit, and share the follow-up to my
2017 Kindle book, *ABC Your Way from Danger to
Opportunity: Spiritual Activism in Changing Times*. Now is
the perfect time for *ABC Your Way from Distress to De-
Stress: A Relief Guide for Home-based Workers*.

It is my desire that you will find some tools or coping
strategies to help you navigate this rocky path we all
have been traversing. I have curated these practices
for decades as I traveled from counselor to massage
therapist, Reiki Master healer and teacher,
metaphysician, coach, and appreciator of all things
holistic. I have passed them along to students, clients,
family, and friends. The only difference now is that
these tools are all in one place and have been tailored
to support the millions now working from home.
Now you can try some on for size, plus the
affirmation accompanying each practice. I promise
there is something in this book for anyone working
from home, and many of the practices translate well
in the workplace, as well. Chapters are designed to be
brief, so this book can be read in one day.
Alternatively, I invite you to read and practice a

chapter a day and see what new habits you form in the twenty-six days. You decide what fits into your schedule and lifestyle. I would love to know what you think.

*Note: The guidance I provide in this book comes from past training and experience as a counselor, massage therapist, corporate trainer, natural wellness practitioner, coach, energy worker, aromatherapist, and student of life. Also, Spirit is my best teacher. Please consult a physician as needed for medical issues, as this book is not to be used as a substitute for that.

1 ALIGNMENT

Years ago, I co-instructed a class on Pain
Management at a massage school. Actually, I took
what the gifted lecturer taught the class and assisted
the students in applying the lessons with clients in the
weekly clinic I coordinated for the second half of
their credit. I felt just as much a student as they were.
Although I was a seasoned massage therapist, I
learned so much new information about how we
invite pain through our diet, posture, habits, gait, and
positions while driving, eating, watching television,
sleeping, and sitting at our desks. One memorable
lesson was to always sit in a meeting, an auditorium,
at a desk, etc. with your dominant eye facing the
speaker. When we do, we lessen eye strain and avoid
that slight turn to see the object or person of
attention more fully. When we make that turn of our
neck or body, we can do so for a long period of time,

lasting the duration of the speech, performance, or work task. As a result, our neck and or body moves out of alignment, resulting in discomfort and even pain.

As a rule, keep your ears, shoulders, and hips in alignment with each other. Test it out. Sit at your computer workstation as you usually would. Are you facing the screen directly, or are you turned in some way? Are your ears, shoulders, and hips in alignment, or are you hunched forward in "tortoise-head" position, with your ears leaving your shoulders and hips behind? You can use this quick and easy test as you scroll on your phone, drive, watch television, lie down in bed, and more. But because teleworkers spend so much screen time with the computer, we run the risk of spending hours in positions that we do not realize bring on pain until it arrives with a vengeance.

What can you do to return to alignment? As any yoga teacher would say, "open your chest." Sit up straight, move your shoulders back as if your shoulder blades are trying to meet and have an intimate conversation, notice your chest sticking out in pride of your attention to your needs, then slowly release. Are your ears, shoulders, and hips all in alignment? Repeat this self-correction again if needed, as well as multiple times a day to retrain your body to support you in a return to alignment.

Affirmation: *I am in alignment with my highest good...and within my body.*

<h1>2 BREATHE</h1>

In my previous book, *ABC Your Way from Danger to Opportunity: Spiritual Activism in Changing Times*, "B" also stood for "Breathe." I believe if I write thirty-five more ABC books on a plethora of topics, this will still hold true. Conscious breathing is just that important. As I stated in that book, "Breathing calms the physiological responses to stress, and helps you connect deeper, and move forward from a foundation of calm and consciousness." It also can have an immediate effect. Plus, it is absolutely free!

Imagine that you are at your home workstation, have hit your groove, and the doorbell rings--your package has been delivered. Or the buzzer goes off on your clothes dryer. Or your child wanders over and wants a snack. Or the Internet goes out. Or, or, or...Whatever the distraction, you feel your frustration start to rise.

What a perfect opportunity for a brief and powerful
intervention--just breathe.

My favorite breathwork is to use yogic or belly
breathing. Inhale deeply through the nose and feel
your belly expanding out like a balloon filling with air.
Hold the breath for a few seconds, and release
through the nose, feeling your belly deflate and
flatten. Well, at least return to its pre-breath state--this
is not a weight-loss technique! Repeat the breath
sequence, lengthening your inhale, your hold, and
your exhale. Continue until you feel a sense of calm
returning to you. Bruce Banner, one, Incredible Hulk,
zero!

Another favorite method is 7-4-8 breathing. Inhale
through your nose for a count of seven, hold the
breath for a count of four, and exhale through your
mouth for a count of eight. Repeat the cycle three
more times. I first learned this breathing technique
years ago when I was assigned to read a book by Dr.
Andrew Weil during my natural wellness advanced
certificate program. I love that man and this
technique, which is based on an ancient pranayamic
yoga practice to help you gain control over your
breathing. Dr. Weil describes it as a "natural
tranquilizer for the nervous system." I have used this
technique personally, and with clients. I would advise
not using it if you are already tired--it will likely nod
you off quickly. There goes your productivity for the
day!

Affirmation: *I breathe in deeply, and my belly and life both
expand.*

3 CHECK IN WITH YOUR BODY

My years as a massage therapist have cemented what started to come together for me when I practiced psychotherapy--many people are out of touch with their body. "I didn't know that hurt until you started working on it" became a frequent musing of clients laying on my healing table. Noooo, I did not create the hurt with my extraordinarily strong hands--the area in question was sore or painful when attention was paid to it.

I could spend several pages extolling the desensitization of our society, but I will refrain. Instead, I will home in on the lack of body awareness many people experience, and how to get more in touch by checking in with body scanning.

Yoga is a wonderful practice that provides an opportunity for practitioners to tune into the body and scan for areas of tension, discomfort, and pain. I have been a yogi for over three decades now, and I admit that in my early years of practice, I was not as conscientious as I am sure the instructors wanted us to be. Thankfully, my continued practice and years of Reiki training have helped me become quite proficient. I first learned to body scan others in massage school while learning Healing Touch. Both forms of energy healing helped me more fully understand the connection between the mind and body.

I now teach people to tune in to their body, slowly moving from head to toe, or vice versa. Notice areas of pain, discomfort, or tension. Is there tingling or numbness? Breathe slowly into those areas. Did the sensation lessen, or stay the same? You can also check in with your body when you take in food and drink. Did the food feel satisfying? Did your stomach bloat or did gas occur? Did the beverage quench your thirst?

Long hours spent sitting is a prime setup for tension to develop. Take time out during the day to check in with your body to see if it needs to shift, stretch, sip, or practice one of the many techniques I have included in other
chapters.

Affirmation: *I am in tune with my body and all its needs.*

4 Dance

So you think you can't dance? Hogwash! It does not matter if you do hip hop, ballet, ballroom, or river dance. Dancing is a powerful way of moving the body and moving energy. It can help work out the kinks from sitting for long periods of time. It can help energize you during the afternoon slump. And it can spark creativity when you have a mental block. For years I held what I called the "Tonya Parker Dance Party" during breaks when I first started working primarily from home. I created a fast-moving play-list from the 80's--my favorite big hair and big shoulder-pad era. Oh, the joy and release as I shook my groove thing while I got jiggy with it.

Why wait for your break? Who says you must sit still to take in information? Go on mute during that conference call and drop it like it's hot...or at least lukewarm. Even if you are in a Zoom meeting, if you can disable video, you can stand and two-step back and forth as you listen. Put some shoulder and hip into it. Plus, what a great way to burn calories from that glazed stuffed pastry and sugary super grande hazelnut mocha latte you passed off as a nutritious breakfast!

Beyonce who? Gregory who? Fred who? Jennifer who? Mikhail who? Martha who? Insert your name right here and claim that you, yes, YOU, are the baddest dancing machine who ever stepped foot into your home office!

Affirmation: *I move and groove with rhythm, grace, and ease...or at least enthusiasm.*

5 Essential oils

Aromatherapy is an ancient system of holistic healing using aromatic plants to affect the mind, body, and spirit. Years ago, on the Monday following my intensive, weekend-long medicinal aromatherapy certification course, I received repeated comments from colleagues about how good I smelled. I was not wearing perfume, cologne, or essential oils. The essential oils, made from resins, roots, leaves, bark, stems, flowers, fruit, and seeds of plants, were still in my system from a weekend of testing and using. It was all legal, I promise! Not only do essential oils smell amazing, but they have several proven benefits, including alleviating stress, anxiety, depression, and insomnia. Some are rejuvenating, and address certain ailments such as arthritis, colds, flu, and sinus conditions.

Working from home can be incredibly stressful,
especially if you have children learning virtually
alongside you, if you or a loved one have experienced
physical illness or injury, or you have been watching
too much of the news! Some stress-relieving essential
oils include lavender, ylang-ylang, and rose. Citrus oils
are also great stress-relievers. I make use of a variety,
including sweet orange, tangerine, lemon, lime,
grapefruit, bergamot, and neroli. I keep a roll-on of a
combination of citrus oils on my desk for quick use.
If you start to feel the stress getting to you during
your workday, try the following tip: place 5-10 drops
of one or more of the oils listed above in a small pot
of water; designate this pot for aromatherapy use
only. Simmer the water and oil mixture over the
course of the next couple of hours, making sure to
refill the water when it runs low. The oils will diffuse
throughout the area. You can achieve the same effect
if you have an electric aromatherapy diffuser or one
using a tea light--as long as some heat source helps
the oils to separate from the water and diffuse
throughout the air.

If you feel sluggish when you arrive at your
workstation, after lunch, or towards the end of your
workday, try this simple aromatherapy remedy I call a
"smellie" to give yourself a boost: place on a napkin
or folded paper towel, two drops of either rosemary,
peppermint, spearmint, eucalyptus, patchouli, or one
of the citrus oils listed above. Close your eyes, bring it
to your nose without touching the oils to your face,
and inhale deeply for a few seconds. You can repeat
this every few minutes, but you will still get the
benefits of the smellie if it just sits on your desk.

Finally, if you like to operate with ease and grace, just purchase a lava stone bracelet. Lava stones are small round beads that are rough but look spongy. Placing a drop or two of essential oil on the stones in the bracelet will diffuse the scent for about two to four hours. This method takes the oil and its properties with you wherever you go. I gave my mother a lava stone bracelet when she was bound to the bed during sixteen months of home hospice care. When I visited her, I would pull out my oil case and place drops on her bracelet. She liked geranium and lavender. You can choose oils with fragrances you enjoy or properties to support you.

Affirmation: *I am in harmony with nature and all her sacred gifts.*

6 Feng Shui Your Desk

When I first embraced holistic living, I discovered
Feng Shui. My discovery was long before anyone ever
heard of Marie Kondo or even Netflix. Feng Shui is
the Chinese art of placement, which integrates the
tidying and organizing that Marie Kondo inspires.
This ancient tradition has so much to offer us all; I
have interviewed practitioners on my podcast, Mind
Body & Soul Food, twice, and I always book one for
my women's weekend retreat.

Feng Shui speaks to harmony between an individual
and her environment. It has a number of different
schools of thought and teachings, and the bagua, or
energy map, is applied to the whole building, a room,
or your car. This bagua designates eight areas that
relate to different life circumstances. They are family,
wealth, career, fame, children, knowledge, helpful

people, and partnership. The individual is the ninth area, which is in the center, representing your overall health and wellness. I love the creativity this practice infuses; there are earthly elements, colors, seasons, numbers, and shapes that correspond with each bagua. You can use symbols to represent certain energies. For years now I have kept two hearts by my bedside because I desire to remain in my loving, committed relationship versus being single. We choose colors and art in our home to evoke the feelings we desire to have. We allow energetic flow through our home with the placement of furniture. We fix broken items as quickly possible. And I try my best to keep surfaces clear, including my work desk. It is a work in progress!

Speaking of the work desk, you can superimpose the bagua map over that, too. Different sections can represent different life areas, and you can select small items to symbolize those energies. I have hung a lucky tassel to my desk lap in my wealth gua, or area. I have a scented soy candle to provide a flame in my fame area. A crystal angel statue adorns my partnership gua--I partner with Spirit in the work that I offer. I have various crystals placed around my desk, though I must admit they are my version of worry beads--I like creating different crystal grids as I sit through Zoom meetings. When I am not conscious, they can become clutter.

I suggest you look up Feng Shui or grab a book on this fascinating topic. Then you can decide what resonates with you and your workspace.

Affirmation: *Energy flows harmoniously to, through, and
around me.*

7 GROUND YOURSELF

Interestingly, when I practiced decades ago as a psychotherapist, I was not familiar with the concept of grounding. I became introduced sometime between studying to become a massage therapist and a Reiki Master. Then I understood the importance of it and was grateful for my natural inclination towards it!

I grew up in rural Warsaw, Virginia. We can just call it "da kuntray" like my friend, Jamila. In da kuntray, I rarely wore shoes in the summer, unless it was time for church, walking about three miles to the local library, or exploring the numerous wooded areas. I used every opportunity to kick off my shoes, and a pair of flat feet are my lifelong evidence. Walking barefoot, especially outdoors, is arguably the best way to ground yourself, connect to the earth's energy, focus on something other than stress, distress, and other emotions perceived as unpleasant. It also helps to anchor you in the present moment. It usually calls on something external to yourself to achieve a grounded state. So I have a radical idea for you: work barefoot. Kick off those heels or Italian leathers and curl your toes and arch your feet throughout the day. Better yet, place them in a tray with sand or potting soil! Too dirty for you? Then how about keeping some medium to large smooth stones under your desk to press your feet on throughout the day?

If none of the above ideas grab you, there is good news. You can practice yoga poses or even take a few minutes to visualize roots connecting your feet to the Earth. Unless you are working outside, you may not be able to take a quick break to go outside and hug a tree. However, you can place a plant on your desk and feel its stems or leaves and play in its soil if you feel yourself uprooting throughout the day. If fondling your plant feels weird, then try rubbing a crystal-- black obsidian, black tourmaline, and red jasper are just a few gemstones you can use for grounding. And if you are wondering if there are any normal, vanilla grounding activities, then yes, you can always choose to grab a snack of nuts, seeds, sweet potato chips, or peanut butter on celery. Or diffuse some patchouli or vetiver essential oils. There is something for every inclination.

Affirmation: *I allow the Earth to support and strengthen me.*

8 Help

Although it has been many years since I have practiced as a counselor, my helping skills have stayed alive and well outside of the mental health centers and hospitals where I practiced. Therefore, I am very aware of the increasing stressors that have been introduced or uncovered within the past year. With those stressors comes a need for us all to be able to identify when we may be feeling overwhelmed, sad, angry, hopeless, alone, etc. Perhaps you feel more stress in your body. You may feel extra irritable. Or you may notice changes in your sleeping or eating patterns. Whatever the feelings, a great option is to seek help from somewhere to deal with them.

Employee Assistance Programs (EAP) are alive and well in this time of telework. Just because your workstation may have moved to inside your home, does not mean you cannot take advantage of the sessions your EAP plan may designate. For those working from home who do not have access to an EAP, there are numerous counselors available via videoconferencing to provide support, insight, and tools to help you cope during these challenging times.

"What if I don't want to talk to a counselor?" This is a fair question; I have certainly encountered many people who choose not to take this route. I counter that question with a reminder that help can come in many forms. For example, you can call on your F Team-- family, friends, and faith leaders--all of whom can provide a listening ear, a different perspective, and some suggestions on how to cope. No matter the option you take, the emphasis is not becoming siloed in your experience, where social distancing turns into emotional distancing--from yourself and others.

Please do not wait until a crisis comes. Be proactive and seek help sooner rather than later.

Affirmation: *I ask for the help I need.*

9 INTENTION

Anyone who has followed any Law of Attraction book or article will know that intention serves as a powerful force for manifesting what you desire. Focused intention takes you out of a state of randomness, haphazardness, and overwhelm and takes you from where you are to where you want to be. It is a very conscious mental process that calls on forethought and taps into a sense of commitment and accountability.

If you have a to-do list that causes your heart to palpitate or a headache to seep up your neck, then think about starting your day, or at least your time at your workstation, with a few minutes of intention setting. Breathe and allow yourself to enter into a positive vibration or mindset. Assess what it is that you want to accomplish for the day and become truly

clear about it. Then create an intention statement and
spend a minute or so tapping into a sense of what it
will feel like to accomplish it. Then speak it aloud, at
least once. For extra credit, you can create a
screensaver on your desktop, laptop, or phone to
scroll that message. Or you can scrawl it on a post-it
note--but you get fewer points if it is messy. Here is
an example:

*At the end of my workday, I give thanks because I: 1)
acknowledged receipt of every email; 2) answered phone calls
only during prescribed work hours; 3) completed Project X; 4)
danced off-video during my 1:00 PM Zoom meeting; and 5)
stretched every 1-1.5 hours. OSB!*

Notice how my statement affirms what I want versus
do not want. It also eliminates words like "try" or
"hope to" --it is definitive. And I also created it as if it
has already happened. If you are wondering what
"OSB" means, it is "or something better." I always
leave room for the universe to step in and redirect me
for a higher purpose. Perhaps Colleagua calls and says
"I'd like to take on that last part of Project X" or you
felt guided to pick up the phone on your lunch break
and you learned you received a $100 gift card for last
month's customer service. I always stay open to the
OSB's!

Affirmation: *I continuously see the results of my focused
intention.*

10 JAW RELEASE

Over the course of two decades, I have frequently come across employees in corporate massage settings reporting migraines and/or tension in their neck, only to have an aha moment when I began to massage their jaw. There are many folks grinding their teeth at night, or even during the day, with no idea of its impact on their body. My palpating fingers have felt that impact, over and over.

Jaw tension can create dental issues, as your dentist will tell you. Ever heard of TMJ or TMD? You may have picked up on it yourself, unconsciously rubbing your cheeks, or hearing a clicking sound in the joint. You may have experienced some difficulty chewing, or even felt your jaw lock up. But jaw tension is not limited to your mouth and cheek area--it also can seep both up and down, leading to facial pain, headaches,

and the proverbial pain in the neck--and shoulders.
What can you do about it beyond consulting your
dentist and wearing a mouth guard?

As you work throughout the day and follow Chapter
C -- check in with your body--remember to notice
your jaw. Mobilize and stretch the joint by slowly
opening your mouth as widely as you can, and slowly
closing it; repeat a couple of times. You can take the
palms or knuckles of both hands and slowly press
them into the groove of your jaw as you open and
close; you should feel the movement directly under
your hands. Breathe deeply into any feelings of
discomfort. Then, I invite you to gently pat yourself
on the cheeks, using your palms to make nice, in case
your jaw caught an attitude from your extra attention.

One last note--if your dentist prescribes you use a
mouthguard, consider wearing it while you work
when you have stretches of time in which you are not
required to speak. We want to make your jaw jolly
again.

Affirmation: *My face is serene and relaxed.*

11 KEYBOARD ETIQUETTE

Because so many people are working from home now, we have fewer in-person conversations. But not every home-based worker is videoconferencing. Lots of us still rely heavily on the tried-and-true method of emailing, and to a certain extent, texting. Our computer and phone keyboards see a lot of action, and we would be wise to follow some rules of etiquette.

Unfortunately, much of true communication is lost if we are not present to hear nuances in tone, read body language, and feel the energy of the person with whom we are speaking. Miscommunication can lead to misunderstandings and all sorts of mayhem. And we know from Allstate commercials that we want to avoid Mayhem!

Here are a few keyboard etiquette tips to remember before you send off that next written communication.

1. Email or text as if you are writing a letter. PLEASE DO NOT USE ALL CAPS! No one likes to be yelled at.

2. Make texts brief and leave longer communications to emails.

3. If you need an urgent response to an email, text the recipient(s) to alert them of the email.

4. Do not assume everyone is checking messages as frequently as you.

5. Double check to whom you are sending a message—it could save on confusion...and embarrassment. That mid-day picture with the come-hither look meant for your boo will not fly well in the corporate world-- and it may even end up on Twitter or Instagram!

6. If you become triggered by what someone has written, follow Chapter B guidance and consciously breathe for a few minutes before responding. Then assess how you would feel receiving your message and adjust accordingly.

Remember, no weaponizing your fingers!

Affirmation: *The intention of my communication aligns with the impact it makes.*

12 LAUGHTER

Everyone has heard that laughter is the best medicine.
My dear friend, Savitri Khalsa, is a Laughter Yoga
teacher, and I have become a true believer after
experiencing several of her classes. Laughter has been
proven to help release the body's natural feel-good
chemicals that fight disease. It also helps to reduce
stress, which is a good thing, since we can list
numerous conditions that are created or exacerbated
by stress. Plus, it brings down our heart rate, our
blood pressure, and relaxes our muscles. The massage
therapist in me approves.

When life starts to feel heavy, take time to lighten up.
Reminisce about a funny experience. Make crazy faces
at yourself in the mirror. Phone a friend--at least one
that can make you laugh...no Eeyores or "Bad Luck"
Schleprocks allowed! Do a web search for good jokes

or funny cat videos. My dear friend Rev. Dr. Anthony
Farmer recently introduced me to baby laughing
videos. They tickle me pink and blue! Savitri says
YouTube is full of Laughter Yoga clips, as well. Or
you can always fake it til you make it--just start
laughing--your body will have a hard time resisting
the stimulus, remembering what feelings go along
with your turned up smile, your shaking shoulders,
and the chortles emitting from your mouth.

Just remember, do not try this activity during a
conference call where somber news has been
announced. No, not wise.

Affirmation: *Laughter is a powerful medicine to be taken by
mouth, multiple times a day.*

13 MASSAGE

What kind of massage therapist would I be if I shared
some other tool for the letter M? Music and
meditation are truly worthy. However, because I am a
great MT, you get the pleasure of learning massage
tips to relieve tension, alleviate pain, boost immunity,
decrease blood pressure and heart rate, and promote a
better sense of wellbeing while sitting at your
workstation. Plus, you can increase your focus and
computational skills from a few minutes of massage.
It is no accident that so many workplaces have
included massage in their staff initiative programs. I
know self-massage is not the same nirvana experience
as receiving from an actual therapist, but the benefits
of massage do not have to be inaccessible if you are
budgeting, busying or social distancing.

For over two decades I have been telling clients and
workshop participants that massage is the manual
AND mechanical manipulation of the soft tissues of

the body. Manual means hands...sort of. I prevent injury and build stamina by using supported fingers, palms and heels plus the whole hand, soft knuckles, forearms, and elbows. I advise you to avoid using a lot of thumb work--you may not have the strength and you can cause wear and tear injury.

Mechanical manipulation has traditionally referred to "Thumpers" and electronic hand massagers. Now you find all sorts of little massage gadgets in any superstore. I happen to like my creative tools I have at home: pencil erasers (great on palms and on bottoms of feet), rolling pins (rolls out those thigh muscles with ease and grace), spatulas (think drumsticks with a flat base on your muscles), smooth stones (provide pressure into thick muscles), towels (use a seesawing motion on your neck, low back, legs, and feet), and tennis balls, which get a chapter of their own.

When you massage yourself, make sure to focus on soft tissue, like muscles, tendons, and ligaments; avoid working on bony areas like the spine. Lighter strokes tend to calm and relax; deeper and faster strokes can energize. In general, make sure your strokes move toward your heart, to help with circulation. Incorporate massaging with stretching and breathing. Use a tool if you cannot comfortably reach an area; I keep a couple on and under my desk, for convenience. Make sure to show love to your hands and fingers when you are done. You do not want to develop arthritis from a technique which treats that very condition. I speak from vast experience.

Affirmation: *My hands have the power to heal.*

14 NATURE

Being outside in nature is one of the most loving, healing gifts we can give to ourselves. The vitamin D from the sun boosts our immune function and provides a host of benefits. We engage in a reciprocal relationship with the trees and plants--we breathe in oxygen that they breathe out; we breathe out carbon dioxide that they breathe in. Hearing the sound of the wind rustling leaves, the birds chirping, and viewing the beautiful colors of flowers and leaves brings such peace to so many. Walking in nature is a wonderful way to ground yourself.

Suppose you find yourself stuck to your desk chair like Velcro. Your eyes are tired from looking at the screen. You are tired of being in one meeting after another, staring at Hollywork Squares contestants on Zoom. Step outside and get an inoculation of nature.

Even five minutes can be a powerful dose. Here is one scenario of how to experience it:

Walk to a spot on the grass or dirt and close your eyes.

Breathe in deeply, using the belly breathing you learned in Chapter B. Notice what you smell.

Listen to what sounds you hear--eliminating man-made noise, what sounds chime in from nature?

Notice how the Earth feels under your feet--firm, soft and springy, rocky?

Now open your eyes and look around at nature's expressions. Note any trees, flowers, bushes, rocks, animals, clouds, sun, or precipitation.

Give thanks and return to your workstation.

In the event you are experiencing high pollen count, torrential downpours, a Snowmageddon event, or smog, feel free to shift to plan B, and bring the outdoors in. Appreciate any indoor plants, rub one of your crystals, inhale some of your essential oils, or turn on that screensaver picture of the water around Aruba, the red rocks in Sedona, or the running of gazelles from your Kenyan safari. It is not the same, but it does help to evoke the feelings that you may get when you are actually in nature.

Affirmation: *I take time to appreciate nature and all her expressions.*

15 ORGANIZE

I genuinely believe that our inner thoughts reflect our
outward expression. Therefore, if your workstation
looks like a disaster zone, what is that saying about
the state of your thoughts? So, the old question of
"which came first, the chicken or the egg" comes up.
In this instance, do you ponder, "clear my thoughts
first and my outer environment will straighten up," or
"straighten up my outer environment and that will
lead to more organized thoughts?" I believe either can
work. However, since I am not wearing the hat of a
counselor anymore, I will speak to you as a
metaphysician and holistic health professional: take
the steps to organize first and check in to see how it
makes you feel. Are you breathing easier? More
focused? Able to complete tasks in a timelier way?

Other ways to set your head and workspace up to
support success include:

1. Do not work from the bed on most days. In all transparency, I work from the bed at least once a week, when my energy feels low or if I need a break from my desk. The bed is not the ideal workspace physically or energetically. It is more challenging to follow the other guidance I include in this book. And, trust me, you will not be as productive.

2. Put house duties on your calendar. Working from home may come to equate to handling household tasks during work time. More distraction, less focus, and increased likelihood of more frustration. However, if you want to book your dinner prep, changing out laundry in the washer and dryer, and placing your grocery order onto your calendar, you get to see how your time is used, and if it feels more integrated into your workday.

Affirmation: *I organize my inner and outer worlds.*

16 PROGRESSIVE MUSCLE RELAXATION

Sitting at a desk is a full-body impact. Your eyes get
tired from the strain. Your neck and shoulders can
slope forward, causing strain. Your hands and fingers
are often typing or writing, causing strain. Your butt
is in a chair for a long period of time, causing--you
guessed it--strain. Our knees may lock, and our feet
may fall asleep as we sit for a prolonged time.
Additionally, during these sitting marathons, we
weaken our glute muscles and over contract our hip
flexors, running from deep in the belly to our pelvis,
so that when we stand up, we may resemble Cro-
Magnon Man, hunched over until our back helps us
to stand erect again. Etcetera, etcetera, etcetera.
Gratefully, there is a technique that can address all of
that and more in 5-ten minutes or less, unless you
want to experience it longer.

Progressive muscle relaxation is a deep relaxation technique that has been shown to relieve stress, anxiety, and chronic pain. It combines breathwork with contracting and releasing your muscles, one group at a time. It may feel counterintuitive to purposefully tense up your muscles, but it truly serves to relax them. I use this technique often for myself, and with corporate and private clients who enter into my Virtual Relaxation Station. I will share a simple regimen that you can personalize for yourself. I like to integrate breathwork with mine, though you do not have to. You can hold each contraction for approximately three to five seconds. To save time, you can contract and release both arms and hands at the same time. The same is true for your legs and feet.

1. Sit or lie down in a comfortable position, with eyes closed. Take a few deep breaths, expanding your belly as you breathe air in and contracting it as you exhale. Repeat twice.

2. Begin at the top of your body and go down. Start with your head, tensing your facial muscles, squeezing your eyes shut, puckering your mouth, and clenching your jaw. Hold, hold, hold, hold, then release. Breathe in and out.

3. Tense as you lift your shoulders to your ears, hold, hold, hold, hold, then release. Breathe in and out.

4. Make a fist with your left hand, tighten the muscles in your lower and upper arm, hold, hold, hold, hold, then release. Repeat with the right hand and arm--

tighten the muscles in your lower and upper arm,
hold, hold, hold, hold, then release. Breathe in and
out.

5. Concentrate on your back, squeezing your shoulder
blades together. Hold, hold, hold, hold, then release.
Breathe in and out.

6. Now focus on the chest area, bringing your
shoulders forward in a tight hunch, hold, hold, hold,
hold, then release. Breathe in and out.

7. Suck in your upper stomach area, above the belly
button, hold, hold, hold, hold, then release. Breathe in
and out.

8. Suck in your lower stomach area, below the belly
button, at your hara, or power center, hold, hold,
hold, hold, then release. Breathe in and out.

9. Clench your buttocks, hold, hold, hold, hold, then
release. Breathe in and out.

10. Tighten your left thigh—quads and hamstrings,
hold, hold, hold, hold, then release. Repeat with your
right thigh. Tighten and hold, hold, hold, hold, and
release. Breathe in and out.

11. Point your left foot to contract your calf, hold,
hold, hold, hold, then release. Repeat with your right
calf. Squeeze those muscles in the right calf, then
hold, hold, hold, hold, and release. Breathe in and
out.

12. Flex your left foot to contract the muscles around your shin, hold, hold, hold, hold, then release. Repeat with your right calf and hold, hold, hold, hold, and release. Breathe in and out.

13. Tighten and curl up your toes on your left foot, hold, hold, hold, hold, then release. Repeat with your right foot. Tighten and curl up your toes on your right foot, hold, hold, hold, hold, then release. Breathe in and out.

Continue to breathe in and out at your own pace, expanding your belly on the inhale, contracting it on the exhale.

You may be surprised at the tension you are holding in various parts of your body. The good news is, you can repeat as often as you like, and wherever you like.

Affirmation: *Contraction prepares me for great expansion.*

17 QUENCH YOUR THIRST

I perceive water as the master element. It can take the form of solid, liquid, and gas. It has the power to create and destroy. Depending on the reference, scientists estimate that the human body is made up of between 60 and 70 percent water--mirroring the amount of water that makes up the earth. Just like Mother Earth needs water to keep her functioning, every one of our living cells in the body needs water to keep us functioning, as well. Use water to quench your thirst.

I know as a massage therapist, experiencer of osteoarthritis, and recipient of two low back disc surgeries, that water is crucial to lubricate our joints. Additionally, it helps to flush waste--why I always recommend clients drink extra water after each session; the process of massage helps move toxins from the muscles and water helps flush the toxins from our bloodstream.

Because water is so crucial to the proper functioning of the kidneys, any time someone experiences back pain, I always check first to assess their water intake.

That low back ache may be a muscle strain, slipped disc, tension from too much sitting, or just a lack of water. I can attest to working from home and getting into the groove of my task (such as writing a book or workshop) and realizing hours have passed since I took my last sip or two. Suddenly, I realize I am thirsty, and start swigging.

What I have found to be helpful is to keep water on my desk. Even then, I may not have enough. My best intake occurs when I fill a 32-oz container with spring, filtered, or alkaline water, and have it sit in a visible spot on my desk. I intuitively was drawn to drinking room temperature water decades before my holistic wellness studies told me it was an ancient Ayurvedic practice that promotes better digestion.

There are downloadable apps that track and remind you to drink water--or you can set an alert or take stock if you do a body check-in to see if you feel thirsty. I have also discovered I drink more when I sip through a straw vs. from a cup or bottle. Using a water bottle with a reusable straw is more earth friendly. Whatever tip works for you, make sure you aim for half your body weight in ounces, according to every Naturopath I have consulted. Therefore, if you weigh 160 pounds, the rule of thumb is to drink 80 ounces of water per day. Please keep in mind you may need to increase that if you exercise, receive massage, Reiki, or other forms of energy healing. And if the weather is hot, you may lose water due to sweating, and you will need to replace it.

Extra reminder--soda and juice are disqualified as good hydrators, and you know you do not want the extra sugar and calories. And just because coffee and tea have water in them does not mean they are hydrating fully either. Coffee is a diuretic, so your kidneys will spend time flushing extra sodium and water when you go tinkle. Herbal tea counts if you make it fresh and skip the sweeteners. My late mother used to give her black coffee a break and drink warm water in the morning, another way of supporting our digestion. If you would like to earn bonus water points, eat watery foods, like vegetables, fruits, and soups.

Still not convinced? Water is just too plain and boring? Add some flavor (and nutrition) by adding slices of lemon, lime, orange, ginger, cucumber, or pineapple, or herbs like mint, basil, or cilantro. Or get jiggy with it and use a combo of any of the above. Do not let any excuses to get in your way as you actively quench your thirst during the day.

Affirmation: *Water nourishes every cell, every tissue, every organ, and every system in my body.*

18 REMINDERS

Recently I had the epiphany that I am the target audience for this book. Here I was, looking outside of myself at all the people that I have helped over the years with the information I am sharing. I should have been looking in the mirror. My work has been 100% based from home for the last several months— 90% for the extent of the pandemic. I need to follow all the advice that I have been doling out to you. Although I believe this chapter may be the simplest, it is the most crucial for me. I need reminders.

When I start working on a book or project, or do voice over recordings, I get hyper-focused. I lose all track of time, and I can emerge three hours later and realize the sunlight is waning, my legs are locked, my back is sore, and my bladder is screaming. If I had set some alerts on my phone or reminders on my laptop, they would have served to remind me to stand, breathe, stretch, drink water, and follow the guidance from the other chapters that I have written. Essentially, for me, the success in the other areas hinges upon my success in this one simple area. So, I challenge you—and me—to do that now. Add YOU to your calendar. Make YOU a task. Set YOU as an alert. Every sixty minutes stop working and check in with your body. Stand and allow those hip

flexors to open up. Every 90 minutes, stretch. Create
a break to eat, go outside, dance, or relieve yourself.
Whatever you choose to do, just plan for it. As the
biggest stakeholder to your success, you deserve an
appointment with you!

Affirmation: *I use my tools and resources to help me maintain
health.*

19 STRETCH

As a yoga practitioner for three decades, I am clear about the benefits of stretching. As a massage therapist for over two decades, I am super clear. That is why I have told my clients time and again that they would easily put me out of business if they stretched routinely. And I am here for it! Loosen your muscles, relieve that pain, increase your range of motion, and increase your flexibility.

We consciously and unconsciously contract our muscles on a constant basis. Contraction helps us move. It helps us strengthen our muscles. And it can cause tension and pain. Our muscles were not meant to be contracted in certain ways for long periods of time. For example, when we sit for hours, squint our eyes, furrow our forehead, sleep with a thick pillow, hunch over a keyboard or a sink, or lift heavy objects without engaging our powerful leg muscles -- we invite pain.

I invite you to pay attention to the repetitive movements you make in your work setting. If you have fine movements, like braiding hair, sewing by hand, or typing on a computer, you may be just as at risk for injury as those of you who use your gross motor skills to lift heavy objects, swing hammers and mallets, or massage and lift heavy limbs. You just may be risking different muscle groups in different ways. A way to mitigate injury is to stop and stretch the muscle groups in question.

Here are just a few simple seated stretches for you to ease into to address various muscle groups:

1. Repeatedly squeeze your eyes shut and open them wide over the course of 20-30 seconds.

2. Repeatedly open your mouth wide and shut it for 20-30 seconds.

3. Touch your ear to your left shoulder for a few seconds, then repeat on your right side.

4. Touch your chin to your chest and hold for about 10 seconds.

5. Shrug your shoulders up to your ears and back down. Repeat.

6. Give yourself a tight hug and release to stretch your back.

7. Take your shoulders back as if you are trying
    to hold a pencil between your shoulder blades
    to stretch your chest muscles.

8. Lift your arms up in front of you and reach
    forward as if you are picking apples from a
    tree. Pick about 10-12 for that cobbler you
    plan to make.

9. Lift your arms up over your head and bend
    your elbows. For an extra stretch, gently arch
    your back as you do so.

10. Drop your arms to your sides and take turns
    bending from the waist to first your left side,
    then right. For an extra stretch, bring your
    opposite arm up alongside your ear.

11. Rotate your hips as if you are slowly hula-
    hooping, then reverse direction. You can also
    do this standing.

12. Extend each leg while pointing and flexing
    your foot.

13. Repeatedly curl your toes and spread them
    wide for 20-30 seconds.

14. Open your legs in a wide stance and extend
    your arms out like a cross. You can move
    your arms up to 45 degrees, then all the way
    up over your head.

15. Stand with your feet about hip-width apart.
    Holding onto a surface, step your left foot
    forward and, if possible, bend into a lunge.
    Tilt your pelvis forward so you feel a stretch
    in your right front hip/groin area. Hold for
    about 10 seconds. Bring your left foot back
    even with your right and repeat with the right
    side.

16. Shake everything.

How are you feeling now?

Affirmation: *I move with freedom and fluidity.*

20 Tennis Ball

What is small and round and has a huge impact? If you answered, "a tennis ball," then you win the prize! You still win if you veer off a bit with a racquet ball or pet ball--they can have the same effect.

I have used tennis balls for many years as a tool for self-healing and a demonstration item when I teach self-massage classes. You can use a tennis ball on various places on your body to alleviate tension and discomfort. It is great to work the bottoms of your feet. This is a favorite activity during my amazing virtual chair yoga classes with my dear friend and healing sister, Robin Bell. I keep a ball under my desk for that very purpose. I actually keep mine in a warm, fuzzy sock to keep it from rolling away. Throughout the day, I grab it with my toes and station it under a foot at a time. I roll my foot over it, pressing in at my toes, the ball, arch, and heel of my foot. It stimulates all the nerve endings and reflex points found on the bottom of the feet. I feel the release of tension in a powerful way.

I even double up and place two balls in a sock, tie the sock off, and create a rolling apparatus with a space in between to roll up and down my paraspinal muscles as I balance with my back to a wall. Imagine yourself with your back to the wall, dipping into gentle squats, as the sock-ball tool works out the tension you have accumulated from hunching over a computer screen.

That ball is truly versatile. It comes out of the sock as I roll it around my tight upper shoulders and neck. I use it to loosen up my hands, much like with my feet. Use two at a time to just roll and press using a desk or table surface. You can even roll the ball up and down the tops of your thighs.

Test it out. See what you think. Just "have a ball" with it!

Affirmation: *Everyday items support my wellness.*

21 UNDO TIGHT CLOTHING

Back in the day I loved wearing tight clothing! Those were the days when it took one easy upward motion to zip up jeans. Long, long ago and far, far away. Fast forward to my becoming a massage therapist in the late 1990's. Scrubs, sweatpants, and elastic-waist pants took over my wardrobe on the days I did not wear the hat--and clothing-- of counselor, community program manager, corporate trainer, or professor.

Why is tight clothing on the no-wear list? I learned in the previously mentioned Pain Management class that tight clothing, tight anything, really, can cause quite a few health issues. These may include restricting blood flow, which makes your heart work harder, and can result in tiredness and fatigue. With limited circulation, you can worsen the appearance of varicose veins and cellulite. Constricting clothing

around the lungs can impact your breathing, leading
to oxidation, which speeds up the aging process. It
also brings on stress and can impact your
concentration. Additionally, you restrict your
movements with restrictive clothing, which forces you
to strain some muscles; for example, tight pants lead
to tight back and hips. And let's not forget our
bellies--tight pants prevent our bellies from
expanding, impeding our digestive process. Our skin
needs to breathe, too, or you may experience redness
or itching. Finally, we women know that we need
breathing room "down there." Tight pants cut off air
flow to the vaginal area and we can develop yeast
infections. So, trade the tight jeans for more comfy
bottoms--if you have a job that requires video
conferencing, folks likely cannot see your lower half.

Now go back and read the previous paragraphs and
substitute the word "pants" and "restrictive clothing"
with "shapewear." I will refrain from using a
particular brand name that we have all come to use as
the universal name of various body shaping
undergarments. You know how we call all tissues
Kleenex and totally negate Puffs and all other brands.
Anyhoo, we women, and some men, have fallen
hook, line, and sinker for this idea that we need to
suffer to look good. And wearing body shapers for
prolonged periods can lead to a path of suffering.
Why? We often wear them every day. We often wear
them for over eight hours at a time. Most egregiously,
we often wear tighter sizes than needed. I invite
anyone who still reaches for Xena (I know you name
your favorite shaper) before heading off to the home
office, let her rest, if not fully retire.

Another note for the ladies: if you have the option,
skip the bra. For that matter, you may also want to
bypass wearing headbands, wigs, tight braids and
updo hair styles. I promise you, I practice what I
preach. When my dreadlocks grew longer and longer
and I put them up out of the way in a high ponytail, I
started developing tension headaches by mid-
afternoon. After thirteen years, my locks had long lost
their luster, and they had to go. With my current
close-cropped cut, I periodically wear bright and
beautiful head wraps. Unfortunately, this option often
becomes more tight and beautiful, and I limit these
wraps to only a couple of hours. And I will let you in
on a little secret: I feel my shoulders, back, and
breasts thanking me for going weeks at a time without
wearing a bra. Talk about freedom! During my
various video conferences, my laptop camera is set
exactly right to have viewers focus on my face--or my
cute headwrap!

Affirmation: *I move fully and freely without restriction.*

22 Volunteer

Why volunteer? Studies over the decades have all shown there are many benefits for those who volunteer, not just for those on the receiving end. For example, volunteering can improve your mood, make you feel healthier, increase your sense of purpose, and reduce your stress levels. If the Mayo Clinic AND Huffington Post report this, it's gotta be true!

Unfortunately, a pandemic can present challenges to volunteering. But it is not impossible. Our home-based workforce may miss all the opportunities previously built in to give back to others through volunteerism. No more food or toy drives, bake sales etc. But Corporate Social Responsibility programs still exist; they just have had to shift a bit.

I recognize we are in a time where many are in need. I have gotten creative with my volunteerism. I donate

my time and talent to create virtual events for my
spiritual community. I joined our Education
Committee to expand our Zoom course offerings to
support not just my chapel, but the instructors and
the various attendees getting benefit from what they
have learned. I also signed up for Be My Eyes, a
program that allows seeing folks to Facetime with
non-seeing folks to help them with simple tasks, like
which carton is the almond milk, or which sweater
they are holding is blue. All of these volunteer efforts
take place from home. I also have left the house,
believe it or not, to donate and distribute self-care and
personal hygiene products to those in need.

And then there is money. You can always donate
money!

Please do not let a pandemic or any other life
circumstance deprive you of giving back to your
community. Whether you lend your time, talent, or
treasure, know that your efforts are appreciated.

Affirmation: *I feel amazing when I help others.*

23 WALK

When I worked in government and corporate settings, I enjoyed getting away from the office by walking during breaks with colleagues, usually during lunch. Walking provided an opportunity to burn calories, clear my head, connect with nature, and connect in a different way with coworkers. I admit that I respond best to accountability partners helping to keep me on task. If you are like me, working from home can be challenging to holding yourself accountable to walking, especially in the cold and rain. Then what are some possible solutions?

Back in the day, before special electronic devices tracked our movement, I used a device that counted my steps. It was quite helpful to alert me when I had not met my goal for the day. In that situation, I began pacing in my house and walking up and down the stairs--usually it was late at night and not a safe time to go outside walking alone. That habit has stayed with me, even if the device has not, and I often get up and walk around the room or walk from my third-floor office to the ground floor, and back up. Still, I can stand to walk more. Ha ha, you get it?

Movement is movement, so walking is only one option. Chapter D reminds you that dance is also an option. You can choose a variety of exercise forms to help you stretch out muscles that have tightened due to prolonged sitting, and to get your heart rate up for cardiovascular health.

Affirmation: *I take the necessary steps to keep up my steps.*

24 eXit on time

Working within an alphabet structure can be challenging when I reach X, so please don't judge me. Just roll with it. I am not asking you to get an x-ray or play a xylophone. My guidance is simple, though not always easy: eXit on time.

Now, I am not here to tell you how to define "on time." It varies for each person, just as how you seek to create work-life balance looks different for each person. But there have been enough studies over the years that have proven that a hamster-wheel work style is not conducive for your health--physical, mental, or emotional. Further studies speak to the impact on our circadian rhythms and melatonin release if we are connected to our electronic devices too closely to bedtime. We know we need our rest for a variety of health reasons.

If you struggle with consistently extending your working day into your me or family time, you may want to include the task to eXit on time in your intention-setting and setting reminders. Or suppose you like working a bit later--then make sure to take a sizable break or two earlier in the day to allow for your evening mindset. That may be a great time to take a long walk in nature, fit in a full workout, attend parent-teacher conferences, or provide homework assistance. If you and your love bunny are both working from home, AND THERE ARE NO MINORS PRESENT, then coordinate your schedules for a little afternoon delight! Oo la la!

Affirmation: *I am balanced in my day, smoothly integrating work and play.*

25 YUMMY FOOD

Quiz time:

You have been working for several hours, start to get
peckish and realize you have not made it to the
grocery store in the past week. All you have are
"ingredients" but no yummy ready-to-grab food. In
this scenario, which option will you choose?

A.   Run out and grab a meal from the closest fast-
food restaurant.
B.   Run out and grab some snacks from the 24-
hour convenience store.
C.   Log on and order from a food delivery
service.
D.   Keep working.

As someone who gets lost in work, I know what it
feels like to skip meals while absorbed in a project. As

a recovering serial dieter, I know the importance of preparation to experience a successful outcome while dieting. Unfortunately, more food establishments provide options that add more pounds than energy or nutrition. It is easy to take the path of least resistance in these circumstances, but the consequences remind us to create another choice: E) Stop and grab the yummy and healthy snacks/meals you have prepared.

Here are some helpful tips to help you keep fueled during the week.

1. Make a trail mix of raw nuts, dried cranberries or raisins, and seeds and keep in a large baggie or container on your desk.

2. Before your work week starts, create little covered containers of parfait, consisting of granola, yogurt (there are dairy-free options now), fresh berries or some other cut-up fruit.

3. Prepare fruit before the work week: slice some oranges, cut up a pineapple, mango, or papaya, and place any bananas getting ripe on your desk so you will remember them.

4. Create food bowl ingredients for a quick grab-and-go lunch over the course of several days: brown rice, quinoa, or gluten-free pasta base; cooked veggies such as onions, mushrooms, carrots, sweet peppers, peas, spinach, broccoli, tomatoes, butternut squash, or sweet potatoes; raw veggies like tomatoes, jalapenos, cucumber, and arugula; black beans or chickpeas, avocado, a bit of feta or other

cheese (vegan included), boiled egg, olives, nuts, seeds, or dried fruit. Top it with a homemade salsa, pesto, or vinaigrette of your choice. Ok, you can use store-bought if you need to, but only the good stuff.

These are just a few ways you can keep yourself fueled as you burn the midday oil.

Affirmation: *I am fueled by Source energy to keep my fire brilliantly burning.*

26 ZEN SPACE

Alas, we have come to the end of our time together. I believe it is synchronous to come to a close with Zen space--it is where I hope you will retreat to when you come to the end of your workday. You deserve it, trust me.

Zen is a form of Buddhism, but as part of popular culture, it has become synonymous with a state of peace or relaxation. Doesn't that sound heavenly at the end of a workday? You do not have to have a special garden, or meditation room, a man cave or she-shed to create a Zen space. Almost any space away from your workstation and other people can suffice. I admit, there are times when I have used my bathroom as a Zen space. I keep essential oils and incense there. There are magazines. If there are other noises in the house, I can turn on the bathroom fan.

If I have time, I will let Calgon (or some of my
natural aromatherapy bath concoctions) take me
away...

Perhaps you have a walk-in closet or a cozy chair in
your bedroom that calls to you when you power
down. It may be your backyard or deck, or a nearby
park. Wherever you choose, just allow yourself to be
fully present in that space, in that moment, embracing
peace, releasing the workday, and preparing to move
forward into what is next on your personal agenda.
This is helpful whether you live alone or have a full
house. It serves as an energetic shower after exposure
to toxic contamination, whether that is a
bombardment of electromagnetic frequencies, coworkers who do not play well in the sandbox, a client
whose issues feel overwhelming, a to-do list that
magically lengthens as soon as you check off a task, or
that project that has you juggling china cups one
moment and live hand grenades the next.

Why not make it a verb? Zen yourself for at least ten
minutes after you complete work as another action of
self-care. Trust me, everyone around you--including
yourself--will thank you for it.

Affirmation: *I set myself up to win after I take the time to
Zen.*

EPILOGUE

In closing, please know that the information I have
included in this book is not an exhaustive list of the
many strategies, tools, and techniques that can
support you as you work from home. Using the
alphabet format meant choosing only twenty-six.
Spirit is helping me learn to edit my normally verbose
self. I could have probably continued into the double
Z's.

Also, the wisdom I have shared will only help you if
you allow it to. Admittedly, change presents
challenges, and we do not always feel up to the
undertaking. It may help to remember that in the
theory of evolution, "survival of the fittest" was not
truly accurate. Survival was won by the most
adaptable. Now is the time to adapt and broaden our
horizons, stretch our capacity, and try out new
behaviors that will support us--mind, body, and spirit.
Now is the time to resist the urge to give in to

feelings of distress, and instead, powerfully choose to use our holistic tools to de-stress. Consequently, I trust that we will emerge as not just survivors of this pandemic, but thrivers.

By the way, right after I completed this book, I found the original version I had searched for last year. As the saying goes, "God's got jokes!"

ABC INDEX

You can find references to the following topics in the
Chapters listed from A to Z.

Nature *E, F, G, N, W, X*

Neck *J, P, T*

Organize *O, R, Y*

Overwhelm *H, I*

OSB *I*

Pain *A, C, J, M, P, Q, S, U*

Peace *E, H, Z*

Positive vibration *I*

Progressive Muscle Relaxation *P*

Range of motion *S*

Reiki *C*

Relaxation *E, J, L, M, P, Z*

Rejuvenation *E*

Reminders *R*

Rest *X*

Restriction *U*

Sadness *H*

Schedule *O, R*

Self-care *X, Y, Z*

Shoulders *J, M, P, T*

Sinus conditions *E*

ABOUT THE AUTHOR

Rev. Tonya Parker has been called a Renaissance
Spirit as she uses her Libra energy to balance a
lifetime of healing work. She has worn the hat of
Mental Health Counselor, Prevention Specialist,
Corporate Trainer, Massage Therapist, Reiki
Master/Teacher, Professor, Conscious Caterer,
Communications Coach, Workshop Facilitator,
Writer and Voiceover Artist. Rev. Tonya has also
been called Therapeutic Goddess, Natural Sistah, and
Throat Chakra Shaman. She simply sums up what she
does as spiritually inspired and guided healing,
teaching, and writing. Her work can be found in
various anthologies; she published the e-cookbook,
*The Tonya Parker Collection: Healthy Eating to a Healthy
Lifestyle*, a meditation CD, *Meditative Morsels: Prayers &
Meditations for Feeding Your Mind, Body & Soul*, and a
young adult novel, *Diary of a Witch's Daughter*. Her first

book in the ABC Series was *ABC Your Way from Danger to Opportunity: Spiritual Activism in Changing Times.*

Tonya produces and hosts Mind, Body & Soul Food, an occasional radio show on blogtalk.com that gives voice to the vision of healers and lightworkers. She offers virtual coaching, holistic classes, and Reiki healing. She is just sticking her toe in the water as she returns to seeing private clients. She looks forward to facilitating retreats and other sacred circles and gatherings later in 2021.

In her leisure, Tonya can be found cooking great food, watching sci-fi and fantasy movies and TV, as well as spending time with her family and friends online, volunteering in her spiritual community online, posing in yoga class online, and beating everyone she can in Words with Friends...online.

9 798722 476333